Print format: ISBN 979-8985401516

This is a work of fiction. All the characters, names, incidents, organizations, and dialogue in this novel are either the products of the author's imagination or are used fictitiously.

The Black Child to Black Woman
Guided Journal

*Accepting the Past and
Flourishing in the Present*

Cheryl Denise Bannerman

This book is dedicated to the best parents a child could ever ask for. You encouraged me, listened, taught me the highest values, and loved me unconditionally. I can still hear you cheering me on from the sidelines every day. I won't let you down, I promise. I will continue to make you proud.

Rest in Heaven. Until I see you again…

Prologue

Your past does not define you. And your circumstances do not define your destiny.

We all come from many walks and life. Our family, friends, social standing, neighborhood, and religion are all things that shaped our lives. They molded us into who we are today.

However, the goal should not be to bury the past but to embrace it.

You can learn from it or hold on to it. But remember, if you hold tight to your past, that is where you will reside.

Why not hold tight to your faith and the one that is always there for you through thick and thin, and who loves you unconditionally – God?

Regardless of your faith or religion, faith is a powerful support system to help you heal.

This journal will guide you in self-reflections about your childhood, teenage years, and adulthood that will encourage you to LOVE the person you've become.

Lesson 1

Childhood

> *Childhood is measured out by sounds and smells*
> *and sights, before the dark hour of reason grows.*
>
> *~ John Betjeman*

 # Introduction

In *Black Child to Black Woman*, Tara Walker talks about her interpretation of 'family' from a child's point of view, including both positive and negative experiences.

 Activity

1. Using ONLY adjectives, describe your childhood.

2. Next, using ONLY adjectives, describe how you feel when you are describing your childhood to someone today.

 *Self-Analysis*

3. Are these two comparisons the same or different? Explain why.

4. Which adjective most resembles you today? Is this what people see? How would others describe you? (Using adjectives only.)

 Activity

If you carry your childhood with you,
you never become older.

~ Tom Stoppard

Can you remember a childhood moment in time when time froze? Describe it in detail, i.e., Was it sunny or raining outside? Were you hot or cold? What were you feeling?

____

____

____

____

____

____

____

____

____

____

____

____

Self-Analysis

Why is <u>that moment</u> significant?

____

____

____

____

____

____

____

____

____

____

____

____

____

____

____

____

____

Putting the Pieces Together

Select all of the 'feeling and emotion' words from question 1. As an adult, when have you experienced these same emotions? Are the scenarios the same or different? Explain.

____

____

____

____

____

____

Can you draw any positives or newfound strengths from that childhood experience and apply it to your life today?

____

____

____

____

____

____

Activity

Tara Walker adored her father. He was her role model. If she could have brought him to school for Show and Tell, she would have. She followed him everywhere, even accompanied him to work occasionally, and helped out in the yard on Saturdays. She admired his strength, knowledge, dedication to family, hard work, and kind heart.

Who was your role model as a child? Why?

 Self-Analysis

Do you carry any of those traits from that role model today? If not, why?

____

____

____

____

____

____

____

As we grow older, our role models simply become 'people we admire'. But why do we admire them? What does that say about our own ambitions in life?

____

____

____

____

____

____

Activity

Finish this Goal Statement:

In the next 5 years, I want to practice being more ____

Why did you answer the way you did? Why is this important to you?

____

____

____

____

____

____

____

____

 # Putting the Pieces Together

How would you begin to start working on this goal? List 3 steps.

1.____

____

2.____

____

3.____

____

Lesson 2

The Teenage Years

> *Trauma is a fact of life. It does not, however,
> have to be a life sentence. ~ Peter A. Levine*

 # Introduction

Tara's teenage years were quite a whirlwind of emotions. From her first love to her first sexual encounter, a frightening experience on her first trip overseas with her dad, to experiencing public school for the first time.

 Activity

What was your most memorable experience as a teenager? This could be anything you feel was traumatic, such as having to walk home from school alone through a tough neighborhood, being bullied, or not having nice clothes like the other kids. Explain why.

____

____

____

____

____

Self-Analysis

Have you experienced anything as traumatic as an adult?

____

____

____

____

Putting the Pieces Together

How has that experience changed your thinking or behaviors as an adult, if applicable?

Nothing in life is to be feared, it is only to be understood. Now is the time to understand more, so that we may fear less.

~ Marie Curie

Self-Analysis

Has any experience as a teenager changed your personality or how you respond to people and situations?

____

____

____

____

____

____

____

____

____

____

____

Where do you think you would be today if you never had that experience?

Repeat this affirmation in the mirror 5 times every morning for a week:

My past does not define me.

I am bigger than my past.

I forgive those who hurt me and will embrace the present and all that I have.

My future is bright, and even more blessings are coming my way.

Use these extra lines to document any other 'life-changing' moments from your teenage years and how they shaped who you are today.

____

____

____

____

____

____

____

____

____

____

____

____

____

____

____

____

Life is short, and if we enjoy every moment of every day,
then we will be happy no matter what happens
or what changes along the way.

~ Gretchen Bleiler

Tara had a near-death experience at a 9th grade graduation pool party at a teacher's home.

Activity

What do you think was running through her mind at that moment when she was gasping what she thought was her last breath?

____

____

____

____

____

____

____

____

____

____

Self-Analysis

If you left this earth tomorrow, what would your final thoughts be about? Do you have any regrets? Explain in detail.

____

____

____

____

____

____

____

Is there room for forgiveness in your life? Who do you need to forgive? (Note: It does not have to be an actual verbal statement to a person. It could be an inner affirmation to forgive and let it go, so you can move on in peace.)

____

____

____

____

____

____

Thinking Back

Think back to the previous question, (*now that you have no regrets);* if you left this earth tomorrow, what would your final thoughts be about?

____

____

____

____

____

____

____

____

____

____

____

____

____

Were your final thoughts of happiness and joy? If not, why do you think that is? Perhaps there is something missing from your life? Or maybe you need to spend time alone looking within and healing.

____

____

____

____

____

____

____

____

____

____

____

____

____

____

____

____

 Activity

What do you like to do when you are alone, your 'self-care' activities? Try to name 10 things.

1.____

2.____

3.____

4.____

5.____

6.____

7.____

8.____

9.____

10.____

Next, create a gratitude list of 10 things you are grateful for.

1.____

2.____

3.____

4.____

5.____

6.____

7.____

8.____

9.____

10.____

The Beginning of Adulthood

> *You control your future, your destiny. What you think about comes about. By recording your dreams and goals on paper, you set in motion the process of becoming the person you most want to be. Put your future in good hands – your own.*
>
> *~ Mark Victor Hansen*

 # Introduction

Everyone follows their own path in life after high school. Some get a job, and some go off to college, and some get married and start families.

Tara learned a lot about herself when she left home and went off to college. Although she was still in the same state, she was on her own and surrounded by new people and an exciting new environment. She was no longer bullied by jealous, spiteful girls but instead became a blossoming flower full of laughter and sexuality. And to top it all off, she had popularity, which she had never experienced as a youth or young adult. She had finally found her voice and she was not afraid to use it and ask for what she wanted.

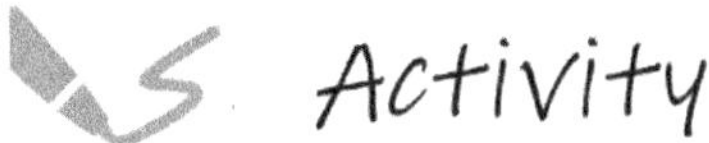

Activity

Think back to those years after you turned 18, a legal adult, all the way through your twenties. What were your goals and dreams at that time? Were they the same dreams you had a child? e.g., to become a firefighter.

> *The thing that is really hard, and really amazing,*
> *is giving up on being perfect and*
> *beginning the work of becoming yourself.*
>
> *~ Anna Quindlen*

 # Self-Analysis

Do you remember when you grew into an adult 'mentally'? When you 'found your own voice'?
What did that look like? Did anyone notice that change?

____

____

____

____

____

____

____

____

____

____

____

____

Putting the Pieces Together

Thinking of who you are as an adult today, are you still using that 'voice'? Or did you lose it somewhere along the way? Can you think of *when* that happened?

 Activity

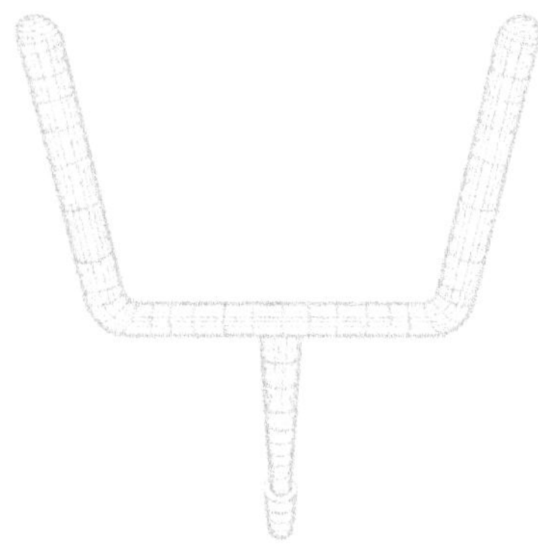

Compare your goals as a young adult to your goals today.

My goals as a young adult…	My goals as an adult today…

Self-Analysis

Do you see any past influences from family, religion, or childhood experiences, etched into the goals in either column?

What parts of your past are you most thankful for, and why?

> *The most beautiful things are not associated*
> *with money; they are memories and moments.*
> *If you don't celebrate those,*
> *they can pass you by.*
>
> *~ Alek Wek*

 ## Activity

List 5 happy or positive memories from any time in your life.

____

____

____

____

____

____

____

____

____

____

____

____

Putting the Pieces Together

Are you ready to Step Out of the Past and Into Your Present? Repeat this fun affirmation each morning for 5 days in the mirror <u>while smiling</u>.

I'm sorry Past, your time is up.

I'm ready for Blessings to fill my cup.

I'm living in the Present and ready to receive.

All the Future has to give.

I now release the Past from the life today and am ready to take the first step into the Present.

Ready, Set, Go!

Lesson 4

Late 20s and 30s

> *True love is like ghosts, which everyone*
> *talks about and few have seen.*
>
> *~ Francois de La Rochefoucauld*

 # Introduction

Tara Walker is no stranger to pain, tragedy, and love. And more often than not, love and pain went hand-in-hand. What she thought was love, was only the 'honeymoon period', a complete façade. In love, we sometimes want to hold onto those feeling and ignore the 'red flags' that are trying to save us from eventual heartache and pain.

 Activity

Name 10 emotions from the 'honeymoon period' (adjectives only).

Name 10 traits you look for in Mr. or Mrs. Right (adjectives only).

1._______________________

2._______________________

3._______________________

4._______________________

5._______________________

6._______________________

7._______________________

8._______________________

9._______________________

10._______________________

1._______________________

2._______________________

3._______________________

4._______________________

5._______________________

6._______________________

7._______________________

8._______________________

9._______________________

10._______________________

 Self-Analysis

Do you see any correlation between the adjectives in column 1 and 2? What do you think it means?

____

____

____

____

____

____

____

____

____

____

____

Putting the Pieces Together

Do you see any connections to the adjectives in Lesson 1, question 1? What do you think it means?

Think about what 'knowing your worth' means to you. Write your answer in quotes, as if explaining it to Mr. or Mrs. Right.

Name 5 things you would focus on during this time.

1.____

2.____

3.____

4.____

5.____

How would you practice self-care during this time?

____

____

____

____

____

____

____

____

____

____

After you have practiced this for 4-6 months, revisit the question 'Name 10 traits you look for in Mr. or Mrs. Right (adjectives only).' Has it changed?

Now, let's shift the focus to you and how awesome you are!

List 10 things you love about yourself.

1.____

2.____

3.____

4.____

5.____

6.____

7.____

8.____

9.____

10.____

Putting the Pieces Together

Do they match any of the traits you listed you were looking for in a mate? Why do you think this is important?

____

____

____

____

____

____

____

____

____

____

____

____

____

____

____

 Activity

We mentioned earlier you should 'know your worth'. Describe what this phrase means to you.

____

____

____

____

____

____

____

____

____

____

____

____

____

____

Self-Analysis

Do you have anyone in your life, past or present, that demonstrates what you just described? What about role models?

When you are in a loving relationship, do you:

- conform to what your mate likes, putting your wants on the back burner
- stick to your own dreams and goals, or
- is there a mesh between the two?

Explain why:

Putting the Pieces Together

Considering your answer, is there any connection to your relationship with either of your parents? For example: did/do you constantly strive to make them proud of you?

____

____

____

____

____

____

____

____

____

____

____

____

____

____

____

____

If you could change one thing about your mate, what would it be?

____

____

____

____

____

____

____

How do you think they would answer that same question? If you do not have a mate, consider a close friend answering this question.

____

____

____

____

____

____

____

If you were being honest with yourself, and you know 'where in your past' that behavior was stemming from, what would you list as the root cause of that behavior or trait?

____

____

____

____

____

____

____

____

____

____

____

Working Adults

> *Hard work spotlights the character of people: some turn up their sleeves, some turn up their noses, and some don't turn up at all.*
>
> ~ Sam Ewing

 # Introduction

This lesson is about the responsibility of holding a job as adults, what it means to us, and how to split our work life with our personal life to avoid burnout.

Tara held many jobs as an adult and was inspired by her parents' work ethic. Her mother and father worked very hard to live middle class and raise their four children. And Tara or her siblings never wanted for anything.

Later in life, her parents started their own business out of their home, and so did Tara later in her adult life.

There was one instance where her co-workers betrayed her, and she ended up quitting her job.

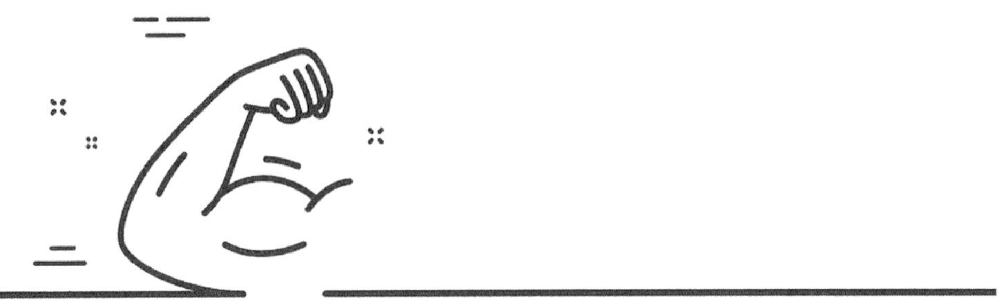

 Activity

Have you ever experienced betrayal on the job, or perhaps any type of betrayal from someone you trusted, that somehow affected your job? How did that make you feel?

____

____

____

____

____

____

____

____

____

____

____

____

____

Self-Analysis

Have you ever faced that person who betrayed you to tell them how you feel? Why or why not?

____

____

____

____

____

____

____

____

____

____

____

____

____

____

____

____

Write exactly what you would say to them:

____

____

____

____

____

____

____

____

____

____

____

____

____

____

____

Putting the Pieces Together

Now contemplate your current job. How does it compare to your goals and dreams from the previous lessons?

____

____

____

____

____

Do you think you are where you are supposed to be in your life right now? If not, what's holding you back from achieving those goals and dreams?

____

____

____

____

____

____

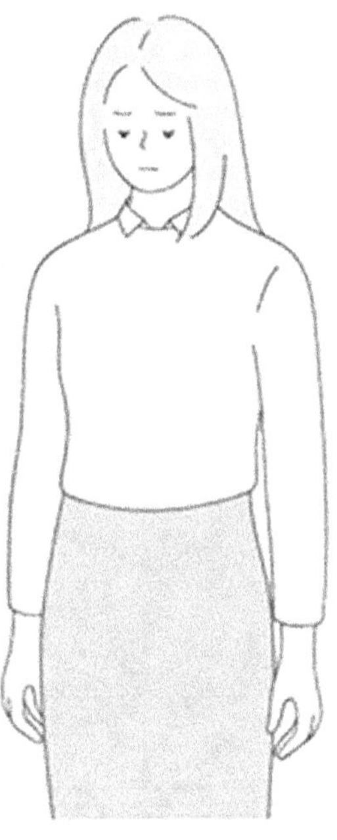

Are there any traits about yourself from the previous lesson that you think are holding you back? What would you like to improve upon?

 ## Activity

List 3 small steps you can take to move you closer to where you think you should be right now in your career. i.e., take a class or reach out to a connection.

____

____

____

____

Self-Analysis

If time is stopping you from moving forward, can you name one thing that is taking up time in your life that could be eliminated? Explain how you would do this.

____

____

____

____

____

____

____

Describe work in 10 words.

1.____

____

2.____

____

3.____

____

4.____

____

5.____

____

6.____

____

7.____

____

8.____

____

9.____

____

10.____

____

Were those words positive or negative? If you were doing your dream job, how would the words differ? List 10 words again.

1.____

____

2.____

____

3.____

____

4.____

____

5.____

____

6.____

____

7.____

____

8.____

____

9.____

____

10.____

____

> *Let us realize that: the privilege to work is a gift, the power to work is a blessing, the love of work is success!*
>
> *~ David O. McKay*

Activity

How do you define work/life balance today?

____

____

____

____

____

____

If you were in your dream job and happy, do you think work/life balance would be a problem?

____

____

____

____

____

____

Take the steps to implement work/life balance into your life by analyzing how your time is split, examining areas where time is not well spent, and forcing yourself to set boundaries and learning to say **No**.

Fill in the shapes on the chart below with the steps you plan to take to achieve work/life balance.

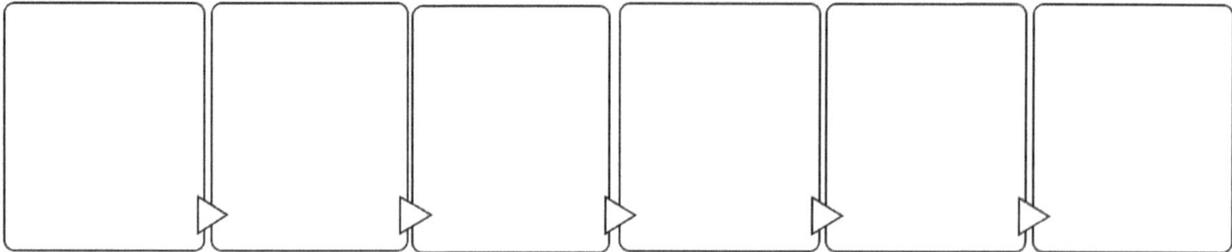

Lesson 6

Secrets and Letting Go

> *There are no secrets that time does not reveal.*
>
> ~ Jean Racine

 # Introduction

Tara had some heavy secrets from her past and present she was holding onto, such as the incident of attempted rape by her cousin.

She also found out some equally heavy secrets about people she loved, such as her first husband who had a porn addiction. He was also abused as a child and inflicted the same abuse onto their child.

 Activity

What secrets do you hold from the past that may be affecting your present?

How do you know they are affecting your present? Is there a trait or behavior making itself known in your life?

Self-Analysis

Holding secrets within and living in the past can cause stress in and on the body.. Most people think it is just mental stress, but it can cause physical stress as well. Research how stress affects the physical body and label each part of the body below with lines and text.

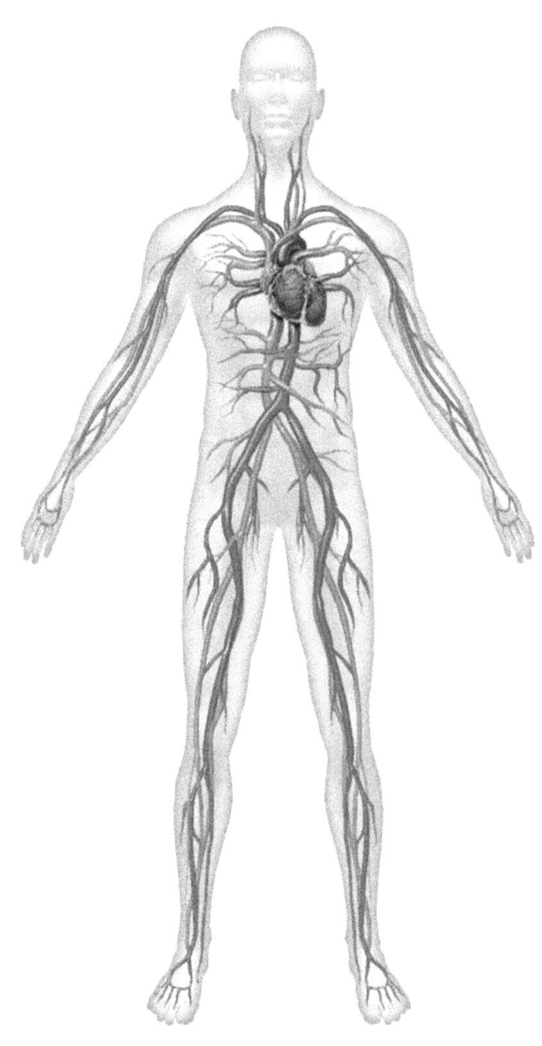

Expand your self-care list from Lesson 2 from 10 to 20 things you can do to take care of yourself.

1.____

2.____

3.____

4.____

5.____

6.____

7.____

8.____

9.____

10.____

Let's talk boundaries. Perhaps you have difficulty speaking up or saying No. This could be at work with your boss or with your mate, or even friends and family.

> *Being a nice person is about courtesy: you're friendly, polite, agreeable, and accommodating. When people believe they have to be nice in order to give, they fail to set boundaries, rarely say no, and become pushovers, letting others walk all over them.*
>
> *~ Adam Grant*

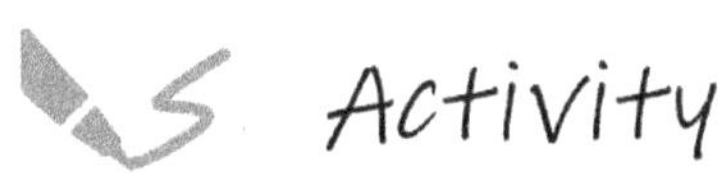 Activity

Do you agree with the quote above? Explain your answer.

____

____

____

____

____

Take a moment to think about what your Boundaries Statement would look like. Consider it to be an expansion of your personal Mission Statement.

Create your personal Mission Statement in 2-3 sentences. Even though a Mission Statement is mostly associated with a business or organization, it can be created for your personal use.

Here are a few resources that may help you:

https://tinyurl.com/52kphevz

https://www.ramseysolutions.com/personal-growth/mission-statement-101

https://tinyurl.com/2wcwbbey

Now, create a bulleted Boundaries Statement with 5 key points. Think about how to prevent others from overstepping your boundaries and how to maintain your work/life balance.

1.

2.

3.

4.

5.

 # Putting the Pieces Together

Repeat this playful affirmation in your head every time someone tries to overstep one of your personal boundaries:

No means No

Off you go

My time is mine

Go get your own!

Owning Your Past

> *Do not dwell in the past, do not dream of the future,*
> *concentrate the mind on the present moment.*
>
> *~ Buddha*

Self-Analysis

How can you concentrate your mind on the present? By focusing on the positive and what you have been blessed with versus the negative and what you don't have. Try to look at the glass as half full instead of half empty.

Start by focusing on the positive and what you have been blessed with versus the negative and what you don't have.

____

____

____

____

____

____

____

Was this one of the adjectives you used to describe your traits earlier? Explain your answer.

Putting the Pieces Together

Start by writing down all the things you were blessed with as a child, a teenager, a young adult, and as an adult today. Complete the boxes below next to each image.

Putting the Pieces Together

Consider the experiences you noted in Lesson 1. Where do you think you would be today without those experiences? If applicable, how would you be different?

Let's revisit our exercise on regrets and forgiveness. Write a letter below to someone you need to forgive.

You want to create your own path,
no matter what situation you're in.

~ Future

Once the hurt and pain of the past is released, you can focus on the present and future. What exciting things do you think the future holds for you?

____

____

____

____

____

____

____

____

____

Part of creating your own path is setting goals. Create your 1-year and 5-year goal plan in the table

In one year, I want to accomplish the following goals…	In five years, I want to accomplish the following goals…

Name a few obstacles that may get in the way of achieving those goals and how you will overcome them.

Obstacle	How you will overcome it

Now it's your turn to create a playful affirmation! Write an affirmation for that obstacle that tries to get in your way.

Lesson 8

Passing It On

 # Introduction

Tara often recalls quotes and stories from her father that kept her strong in the face of adversity, such as not 'wearing her emotions on her sleeve'

 ## Activity

What traditions, beliefs, or phrases are being passed on generation after generation in your family?

In life, we sometimes remember positive words we learned as a youth to propel us forward, and sometimes we even remember the negative experiences to remind us of what we do not want in our lives for ourselves, our families, and even our children.

Being surrounded by drugs and alcohol from within Tara's immediate family throughout her whole life, and attending more than one funeral from a drug-related death, has acted as a repellant for her. It removed the temptation, need, and desire to even experiment with them as an adult, which in turn served her well — ultimately leading to her successful career.

What phrases, quotes, or stories do you often turn to when life hits you hard? Are any of them from your childhood?

____

____

____

____

____

____

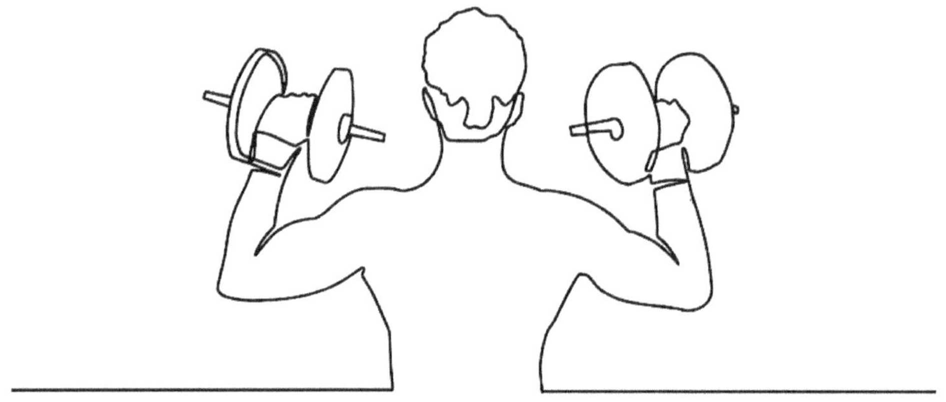

How would you have handled adversities without them?

Self-Analysis

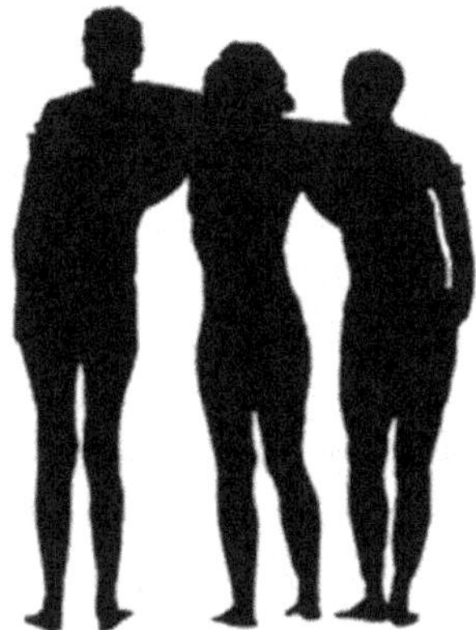

There's a term called 'paying it forward' that means taking kindness others have shown to you or blessings you have received in your life and sharing that kindness or blessing with another person.

Have you ever been on the giving or receiving end of this act of kindness? Explain and detail the feelings you experienced that day. If applicable, how did it change your perspective on life?

____

____

____

____

____

____

____

____

____

Many of us smile and go to work, school, etc. with life pressing down on us inside. We've suffered illnesses, deaths in the family, financial strains, and more. But when someone greets us and asks how we are, we put on a brave face and answer, 'Fine'.

When you greet others, do you ask how they are doing? How often do you wait for their reply and really listen?

Research the term 'active listening'. Now, list 5 or more ways you can be a better listener **and** 'pay it forward' with an act of kindness.

How to Be a Better Listener	How to 'Pay it Forward'

 Putting the Pieces Together

Which item from this list will you implement within the next 2 days? Explain HOW with actionable items.

What happened after you 'paid it forward'? What was the response of the receiver? Was there a change in your mood? Do you think you will do this more often now?

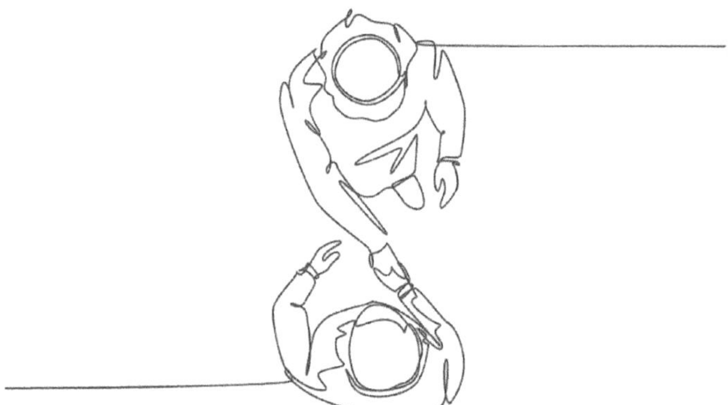

Fill in the blanks below with your own words:

I do not give to receive, I give to ____

____

____

If I could spare 60 seconds to listen when asking 'How are you?', it could change ____________

____

One act of kindness could alter ____

____

Sharing what I have been blessed with makes me ______________________________

____

____

____

____

Lesson 9

Adulting

 # Introduction

Tara learned that adulting was full of responsibility, heartache, joys, and triumphs. Through all of it, she could always rely on her parents to talk to her, encourage her, and most importantly, listen. They were the only two people that loved her unconditionally.

 Activity

The dictionary defines support as "a person or thing that gives aid or assistance" or "something that serves as a foundation, prop, brace, or stay".

What does 'support' mean to you? Describe in detail.

____

____

____

____

____

____

____

____

Who do you go to for support and to listen objectively? Why or how is this person helpful in your life? (Note: This could include a therapist or counselor.)

____

____

____

____

____

____

Self-Analysis

When others come to you for this type of support, how do you respond:

...If you are busy at work?

____

____

____

____

____

____

...If you are going through your own problems?

...If you have time to listen?

Wikipedia states that, 'Active listening involves the listener observing the speaker's non-verbal behavior and body language.'

They note that when responding, there are three steps you should follow:

- Paraphrase: Explain what you believe has been said in your own words.
- Clarify: Ensure you understand what has been said through asking questions.
- Summarize: Offer a concise overview of what you believe the main points and intent of the message received are.

Additional guidelines include:

- Keeping your attention on the message being presented. Remove any distractions such as cell phones or other electronic devices.
- Refraining from thinking about your own response to what is being presented.
- Holding back offering judgement on anything the other person says.

Which of these techniques do you struggle with when listening to others?

____

____

____

____

____

____

____

____

____

____

 Putting the Pieces Together

Name 3 ways you can improve your active listening skills and describe how you will you implement changes.

____

____

____

____

____

____

____

____

____

Add goals related to this improvement to your goal sheet from earlier. Remember, <u>small incremental steps that are realistic</u> can help you achieve your goals more easily.

Lesson 10

The Moral of the Story

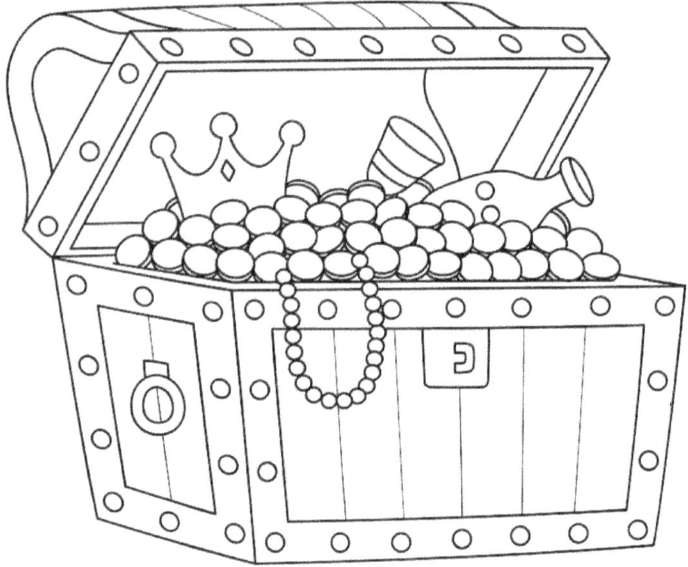

Many stories teach a moral at the end, and often, our own lives do the same. In this journal, you've analyzed every phase of your life, from youth to adulthood. You've evaluated the impact of your youth on your adult life, and documented ways you can be a better person, a happier person, and how to let go and grow into the future you are destined for.

My hope for everyone who has gone through all the steps, is that you can accept the fact that good and bad experiences shape us into who we are today, that mold our personalities and how we relate to others, they build our strength and resilience, and they help us grow.

However, the most important point is that our past is just that – our past. It does not have to impact our present or future. Acknowledge it, understand it, accept it, and live in the present.

Your life is in the here and now. There are wonderful things all around you and wonderful things to come.

The treasures in life are right around the corner, in your future, waiting for you to scoop them up. May you receive all the bounties owed to you.

Take a moment to document the most important thing(s) you learned about yourself from this journal.

____

____

____

____

____

____

____

____

____

____

____

____

____

____

____

____

____

What treasures does the future hold for you? What do you desire for your future?

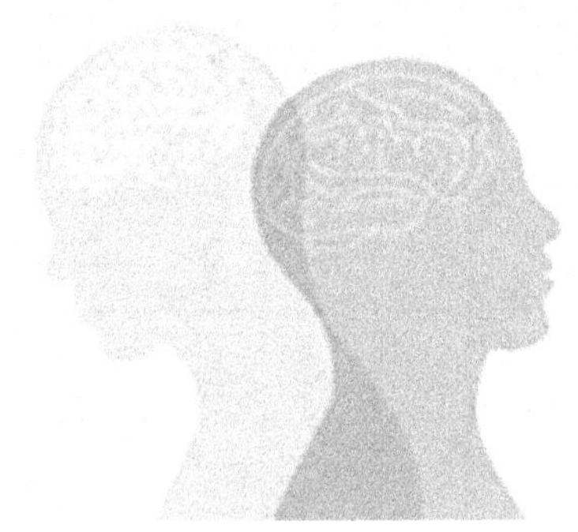

How can you encourage those treasures to reveal themselves? What small changes could you make in your perspective and thoughts? (Tip: Think back to the optimist / pessimist activity.)

____

____

____

____

____

____

____

____

____

____

____

____

____

Write an affirmation or poem about embracing life in the present and your hopes for the future. Alternate activity: Draw a sketch of what you or your life would look like in your new, bountiful future.

Extra lines for additional thoughts.

Extra lines for additional thoughts.

Extra lines for additional thoughts.

About the Author

Cheryl Denise Bannerman is an award-winning, multi-genre author of eight published works of fiction – from cozy mysteries and psychological thrillers to a recent children's book about friendship.

She is the winner of the 2018 Book Excellence Award for her book of poetry, Words Never Spoken, winner of the Best Books Awards in the category of African American fiction in 2020 for Black Child to Black Woman, and 2021 Readers' Favorite Honorable Mention in the Fiction - Urban genre for Black Child to Black Woman. She is also a Semi-Finalist in the MLC Audiobook Awards with a 2020 IMDb Nomination for Book 1 of the Anna Romano Mystery Series, Cats, Cannolis, and a *Curious Kidnapping*.

The author draws her inspiration from life experiences, observations, and lessons. Her goal in life is to keep writing and continue helping victims of Domestic Abuse/Violence, Grief and ANON family groups, and Corporate Health and Wellness groups, to heal through words — encouraging them to 'write the pain' via journaling, and expressing themselves through short stories, songs, and poetry.

When she is not working from her home office on her virtual Training and Development business, she is at the beach watching the waves and weaving words together for her next novel.

Check out some of her other works of fiction at www.bannermanbooks.com

Title	*Category/Genre*
Words never Spoken	*Women's Inspirational/Poetry*
Black Child to Black Woman	*Coming-of-Age/Family Drama*
Cats, Cannolis, and a Curious Kidnapping	*Book 1 of the Anna Romano Mystery Series*
A Bloody Stiletto, Cold Lasagna, and a Bestseller	*Book 2 of the Anna Romano Mystery Series*
Family Ties, Missing Organs, & Champagne	*Book 3 of the Anna Romano Mystery Series*
A Killer's Reflection	*Erotic Psychological Thriller/Serial Killer*
The Gecko Without An Echo	*Children's*